Melancholy River

Hugh Waldock

Hugh Waldock was born into a middle income family in Marylebone, London in 1977. He has lived in many different towns and cities including London, Witham, Essex, Colchester, Berlin Lichterfelde, Kassel Nordstadt, Wuppertal Elberfeld and Cologne Lindenthal. He attended a traditional English public school, called Ipswich School where he passed all thirteen of his high school exams. He went on to study many subjects at music college and university including music, musicology, English, applied linguistics and German both in the UK and in Germany. This period of learning ended with a masters degree in English for Specific Purposes a branch of English Language and Linguistics. During his time at university he taught English in language schools and in companies in the Rhineland and Ruhr area of North-Rhine Westphalia in Germany. He also worked briefly as a countertenor soloist singer. Hugh's writing career began at school when he won a school prize for composing and reading his own poem in a literature performance competition final. Since then he has written two novels and three other publications of which this is one. He is single and enjoys cooking world cuisine for his friends. His life philosophy is very much one of making every side of you work as part of a career.

Melancholy River

This epic poem was partly conceived as a reaction to the pre-Raphaelite painting the Lady of Shallot and submitted as an official piece of GCSE English coursework in 1994. I have extensively re-edited it as a piece of children's literature. The tale would interest anyone with a passion for fantasy literature and children's verse.

It is a traditional fairy tale about the relationship between the water spirit Pippa Boy and the water nymph River Girl that starts off peacefully and ends in tragedy after the intervention of the birds and the fairies. The likeness to the Lady of Shallot comes as a surprise, so I'll keep that place in the story secret for you to discover.

Hugh Waldock

Contents

I

Flowing,

Twisting,

Churning,

Boiling,

Bubbling,

Springs the romantic river born.

A stream,

Crystal clear,

So transparent it isn't there,

An eddy,

A flowing,

Moving,

Living thing,

So shallow that grass grows beneath it.

The spirit of the river can only now be seen

As he turns and flows around

Writhing his lean self

And winking his rainbow eyes.

"Good morrow",

He said to all the world,

"I'm to be the savior of this land

Make me famous in all the world.

Thank the immortal one that that I'm finally alive".

He glided along his innocent paths,

Birds sang of him sweetly,

"Pippa boy",

"River boy",

"God save the river boy..."

And he tipped them with freshwater kisses

"Come, drink,

"Take all. You may."

"Then fly, and soar,

Dance, and play,

Follow me all the way

To wherever destiny takes us".

Dusk-lit chaffy-mellow pastures by,

Waning blue to richer blue

Until a purple sky did see.

The water spirit rested.

He did rest

And at what a more lovely site,

At a moon's dispersal on river's flight?

A gentle breeze,

Ripples too,

Soft and gentle,

Soothing,

Sleep....

II

"The fairies sing a song to you,

A song of love,

On lute and harp,

Golden twinkles,

Bright and blue,

Dancing maypoles,

Dance with you.

Taste this sugar

And taste this stew,

Which,

Little spirit,

Tastes better to you?

Sugar is sweeter,

Love is too,

Find a pretty water-maid,

Use your heart,

A little boy has got to start.

Once you start,

You cannot stop;

Sugar,

Sugar,

Evermore,

Open up your cavern-less store.

Touch it once,

And love,

Love,

Taste it little one,

Love,

Don't leave it thus."

So he took the offer up and ate,

He relished his first bite.

Sweet aromas began to fill the air

And fairy magic swirled and flowed.

"I feel

I've felt a thousand hands,

A thousand touches,

So soft and gentle was that kiss.

Soft and gentle was that kiss my friend,

A hold,

A magic,

A stun,

But what am I to describe it,

Mere words are no satisfaction,

I must seek out more until I find true love."

III

He awoke

In the morning to rise

To red and pinky-sirrus skies.

"Birds!

Fellow tweeters my friends!

We have a quest

To seek a foreign and lonely guest,

'The water-nymph.'

Where does she dwell?"

"Ha, ha, ha.

What tripe you speak!

Don't you mean

Let's play water-nymph?"

"We can't see a water nymph.

What are the rules?

How do you play?

We don't feel like a quest today?

Can we play soldiers instead?

We want to play soldiers,

We want to play now!

Oh, no don't cry little muffin,

Don't cry!

How dare you cry for a woman?"

"Help!

Help me escape!

Fairies, where are you?"

"They are but children

And now I'm a man,

But they are all I have.

What shall I do?

No one wants me to love but you."

A faint echo

Rebounded off the water's edge;

"I am a woman

And they are but children

I have no-one to love but you fairies."

He looked,

She turned,

Her eyes were glass with a glowing diamond centre.

His were shimmering with rainbow tears.

"Hello",

They said shyly to one-another

And laughed

In their underwater transparent bath.

They turned away.

Not knowing what to say,

And then twizzled back to one another again

And looked, and smiled, giggling

As their eyes met electromagnetically.......

Then they actually said it;

A stuttered and love shocked "I.....

Love.....

You..."

Then into thrusting arms they blossomed

Each other's love with kisses.

They laughed,

And danced,

Kissed,

And danced,

Spun,

And danced

Laughed,

And danced,

Then danced again,

And loved,

Or was it danced again,

(I can't remember), seemingly forevermore anyway?

And music played sweet mellow tones of yet more love:

Long,

Drawn out,

Romantic notes,

Ornamented this scene of grace

With swooping and sliding violins

Soaring and gliding trombones

As if arisen to sit on clouds with alien races

And then gradually floating

Down,

Down,

Down,

Until only a single note was sung

And faded into the mists of endless time.

IV

"What a stupid thing to do!

Why does he dance so?

Why does he sing?

Why is his outlook on life so thin?"

"What does he see in *her*,

This golden goose that lays him precious eggs?

Aunty Flo is far more now,

Better legs,

Better hair,

Better breasts,

And bum to spare."

"Daft creatures!

Look into her eyes of diamond fire,

"They transport me to a fifth dimension of love bubbles!"

Here lies her spirit,

Her flair,

Her charming nature so pure

Like a mineral rich stream.

Her vision as wide and reflecting as a lake,

Her brain as submissive as the most seductive of hares

Yet sharp as the hunting wildcat.

Her body is a length of wood

She really would credit me

If I played the carpenter

And carved her to perfection with my hands."

"Oh *smart* lover!

 Oh good*bye*! Oh *go*!

Oh live with your new found *girlfriend*!

We'll soon see how long it lasts,

But no groveling at our feet,

Pippa boy and River girl

When temptation passes your way;

For now we are gone

And when she is too *master.*

You will wither!"

"No, No, Stop, my friends

Do not take offence!

I need you all as well

Here me out

Don't harm me please, I pray!"

"Sorry my dear Pippa boy,

You can't have loved us all as well.

We were your mates.

Now we're just dust,

In the palm of your selfish hand."

"So be it fairies and beastful birds!

But when you grow

You'll understand me then,

When you've ambitions to herald the morning air

Or be a mother hen.

And all you'll ever known is lust

With brewed barley in hand.

That's all you'll ever want to know.

With you

Ignorance of true love is bliss!

Be gone!"

And with that they departed

Up to the palest paw of cloud in the sky,

Wings fluttering,

Beaks piping stubborn-witted songs,

But never once did a single one look back

Through the silent sky

To watch the multi-coloured tears fall

One by one onto the shaded river bed.

V

So it came to pass.

Pippa boy

And river girl

Did live

Love

And marry in splendor.

Crowned monarchs

Of a silent backwater

They dwelled

In a castle of crystal.

Elegant twisting staircases

Of ruby and mother of pearl

Led to four stately bedrooms.

Impressionist paintings lined the walls.

The ceilings were encrusted with emeralds and diamonds

And near to homely fires in bubbles glowing

Stately servants in green gowns were housed

Telling stories of past adventures

Sometimes not so fit

For such a peaceful king to hear.

And so it would have been

If not for the fairies malicious plot.

"They've gone too far!

We've had enough!

It's about time we stirred things up!

Dear birds we know and understand

It's best to act on this underhand.

We'll pay that Pippa Boy back for you

And this is what we'll have to do…"

VI

"Before this night is out

A charm of tears will be cast and take river girl away

To a remote island where she will stay.

Her gills will be cursed away

And replaced by cumbersome lungs of air.

Pippa Boy will observe

But he won't be able to talk to her

And she won't be able to hear.

Her diamond eyes will remain part of her

Along with her golden mane

And pretty visage

She will watch but not see the world beyond

From that tower in which she will lay.

For if she looks on or loves another man

She will spring the trap and die."

Pippa Boy heard nothing of these plans

Until it was too late.

In the morrow morn he woke

To find his love had gone.

Up and down he fanatically searched

He swam over five miles in all.

But there was no sign of a missing lover.

He dropped spent on his lonely throne

As the fairies lavished on his despair...

"Gaze into this seashell gift

We've taken back our daughter."

Lo and behold

An object

Spiral in shape

Appeared on his desk!

He picked it up

And at first it seemed an average thing

Swapped for his life

His meaning and his wife.

When he held and looked into it

An ectoplasmic haze surrounded him

And within it a vision took shape;

It was River Girl depicted in her tower

Lying on a bed of reed

Slow breathing as a wraith.

He knew she was alive

As he could see her there.

He viewed the beauty curve of her body

With its golden section

Like he had done so many times before.

But this time he experienced an acute torture,

Not being able to kiss her.

She didn't utter a sound

But now weaved away tirelessly on her loom.

Mournfully he tapped the shell

To see if it would permit him to enter.

Like in a prison he was ensnared

Upon reading the charm of tears

Inscribed on the base of it.

He wept,

As he already knew their fate.

He wept and wept

And wept and wept

Until no tears were left in him.

Why do this?

Was it not such mythical creatures

Who implant such a desire to love in us?

Why betray *us*?

Why snatch away *his* heart in so sparing a fashion

To constrict the life from his garden of love

Like murderous bindweed?

Had they done the same to her,

That thought he could not bear?

He wished he were mortal

To die and escape the pain of her preciousness

But torture him with his own immortality they did...

Every day he woke to look in her shell religiously,

So that after time

Her name and who she was gradually faded into a concept of 'her'.

Love became fatigued.

What once was ever fonder in her absence

Became the neutron ray that spit them

Into an ever increasing run of new relations

With their own, now stronger gravities.

He could see them wrenching apart.

"One day she saw a handsome boy

Who had liked to play soldiers,

And reminded her of Pippa Boy when he looked in the mirror

And she could resist no more;

She turned on him

With a gaze of mortal lust rather than true love

But she was not allowed it;

As the mirror cracked

Her life snapped

And she began to feel the hand of death.

She knew immediately where she must go;

She felt him come back to her,

"Down to the water",

She said hastefully

Racing headlong downstairs and into his rowing boat moored up on the bank.

She cast herself away from temptation

Back into his arms

To be carried faster and faster by the eternal stream and flow

"Not lust", she said.

"I was and am his true love".

The unchallenged passion fire returned

To the flawless gems that were her eyes.

She died singing,

Singing of Pippa Boy

And of the faith in her first love.

Pippa Boy watched from his vision shell

Then he swam to where the boat had drifted

And supported it laying his arm gently underneath it,

And pushed it with energy on its way

Throwing it like a dart towards heaven.

Slowly it drifted off with her in unconsciousness

Her life ebbing with the tide away.

He blow her a single kiss

Which grew angel's wings

And as it flew towards her cheek

And that messenger played a fanfare on a natural trumpet

It popped as a bubble on her reddened face.

All this was to depict how much he loved her.

The kiss was so strong that it touched her face with soothing magic

The second that she died.

How they had longed for that one last touch

So cruelly, cruelly denied.

20935646R00021

Made in the USA
Charleston, SC
31 July 2013